How Bees Make Honey

by Emily C. Dawson

amicus
readers

Amicus Readers are published by Amicus
P.O. Box 1329, Mankato, Minnesota 56002

Printed in the United States of America at Corporate Graphics,
North Mankato, Minnesota.

Library of Congress Cataloging-in-Publication Data
Dawson, Emily C.
  How bees make honey / by Emily C. Dawson.
     p. cm. – (Amicus Readers. Our animal world)
  Summary: "Describes the process of honey-making from gathering nectar to
  beekeepers harvesting honey and people eating it. Includes comprehension
  activity"–Provided by publisher.
  Includes index.
  ISBN 978-1-60753-012-1 (library binding)
  1. Honeybee–Juvenile literature. 2. Honey–Juvenile literature.
  3. Bee culture–Juvenile literature. I. Title. II. Series: Our animal world.
  SF539.D39 2011
  638'.16-dc22

                                  2010007466

Series Editor   Rebecca Glaser
Series Designer   Kia Adams
Photo Researcher   Heather Dreisbach

Photo Credits
67photo/Alamy, 16, 20 (m), 22 (tl); Catalin Petolea/123rf, 6–7, 21 (b); Corbis/
Tranz, 12, 14–15, 20 (b), 21 (t), 22 (bl, tr, br); Emir Shabashvili/Alamy, 8, 20 (t),
22 (mr); Graham Meadows Ltd/www.gmpl.co.nz, 4, 21 (m); M.antonis/Shutterstock,
1; Martin Poole/Getty Images, 18; Scott T. Smith/CORBIS, cover

1224
42010

10 9 8 7 6 5 4 3 2 1

Table of Contents

nectar

Bees make honey. Bees
need nectar to make honey.
Bees eat nectar and
honey. They eat pollen, too.

Bees get nectar and pollen from flowers. They fly from flower to flower getting nectar and pollen.

pollen

beehive

The bees take the nectar
and pollen back to
the beehive.

Bee Dances

near
the hive

far from
the hive

At the beehive, the bees dance. Their dance shows other bees where to find the flowers.

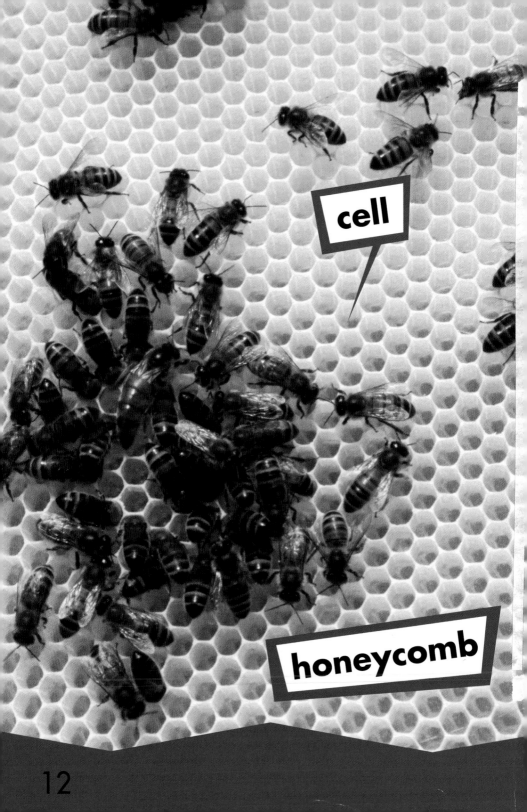

Bees in the hive make honeycomb to store the nectar. Each cell in the honeycomb has six sides.

Bees put nectar into the honeycomb. They beat their wings to make it dry. When the nectar is dry, it becomes honey.

nectar

15

beekeeper

Beekeepers take out the honeycomb. They scrape off the honey. They put it in jars for people to buy.

People use honey to make their food sweet. Do you like to eat honey?

Picture Glossary

beehive
a nest where bees live, build honeycomb, and make honey

beekeeper
a person who raises bees and harvests their honey

cell
a small section of honeycomb with six sides

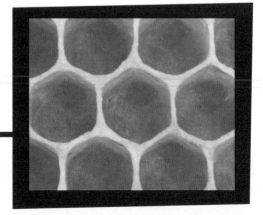

20

honeycomb
a wax frame made by bees, used to store their pollen, honey, and eggs

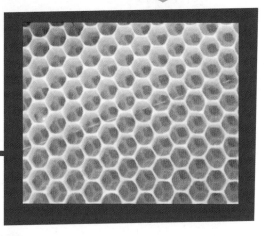

nectar
a sweet liquid that bees collect from flowers, put into honeycomb, and turn into honey

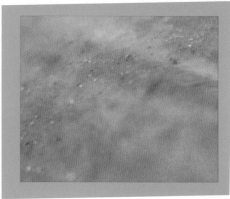

pollen
tiny yellow grains made in the middle of flowers

21

What Do You Remember?

The steps for making honey are all mixed up.
Do you know what the right order is?

Beekeeper takes out honey.

Put nectar in honeycomb.

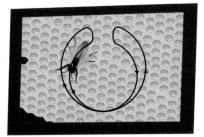
Dance and tell the
other bees where to go.

Go back to the hive.

Dry nectar with wings.

Get nectar and pollen.

22

Ideas for Parents and Teachers

Our Animal World, an Amicus Readers Level 1 series, gives children fascinating facts about animals with lots of reading support. Photo labels and a picture glossary reinforce new vocabulary. The activity page reinforces comprehension and critical thinking. Use the ideas below to help children get even more out of their reading experience.

Before Reading

- Ask: What do you know about bees and honey?
- Discuss the cover photo and the photo on the title page. What do these photos show?
- Look at the picture glossary together. Read and discuss the words.

Read the Book

- "Walk" through the book and look at the photos. Ask questions or let the child ask questions about the photos.
- Read the book to the child, or have him or her read independently.
- Show the child how to refer back to the picture glossary and read the labels and diagrams to understand the full meaning.

After Reading

- Use the What Do You Remember? activity on page 22 to help review the text.
- Prompt the child to think more, asking questions such as *Is it important for the bees to tell other bees where to get the nectar from? Why? Is it important for the bees to make a place to keep the nectar in? Why?*

Index

Web Sites

Bee Buzz For Kids
http://photo.bees.net/kids/

How Honey is Made and Produced: Slideshow
http://www.champlainvalleyhoney.com/slideshow.htm

National Geographic: Honeybee
http://animals.nationalgeographic.com/animals/bugs/honeybee/

National Honey Board: Cooking with Honey:
Recipes for Kids
http://www.honey.com/nhb/recipes/category-results?category_number=8